FIND A WAY

Unlocking Your Best Self

Tim Carter
Foreword by Todd Durkin

No part of this publication may be reproduced, stored in a retrieval system, or transmitted in any form or by any means—electronic, photocopying, recording, or otherwise—without prior written permission, except in the case of brief excerpts in critical reviews and articles. For permission requests, contact the author at trcarter23@gmail.com.

All rights reserved.

Copyright © 2024 Tim Carter

ISBN: 9798337792484

The author disclaims responsibility for adverse effects or consequences from the misapplication or injudicious use of the information contained in this book. Mention of resources and associations does not imply an endorsement.

To my beautiful wife and best friend, Riley:

Thank you for making me better every day, for loving me wholeheartedly and unconditionally and standing next to me each step of the way on this unbelievable journey of life.

Sorry I wake you up at 2:00, 3:00 and 4:00 in the morning to go and start my day.

I love you and will always love you.

—∞—

To our first born and gracious gift from above, Sloane:

Thank you for the unending love and joy you've brought to our lives. Since the moment you were born, you have made everyone better around you.

Thank you for sharpening your mommy and daddy.

I can't wait for you to read this one day.

—∞—

To my mother and father, Chris and Rob:

Thank you for raising me to show compassion, care for others and to see the good in all things. And, for creating and setting the standard of excellence.

—∞—

To my sister, Amanda:

Thank you for your heart of gold and the example that you set for others.

Table of Contents

Foreword by Todd Durkin 1

#GetAfterIt 7

Find a Way 13

Chapter 1: Go Deeper 19

Chapter 2: Iron Sharpens Iron 35

Chapter 3: Purpose 47

Chapter 4: Be Persistent to Be Consistent 53

Chapter 5: Do It Anyway 63

Chapter 6: Suck it Up 73

Chapter 7: Locked-In 81

Chapter 8: There's Always Another Level 95

Quick-Hitters 105

Acknowledgements 117

About the Author 123

Foreword

"Live a life worth telling a story about...what's your story?!" is something I've been saying for a long time. I believe that most people who have tasted adversity, setback, failure, or challenge, often have an incredible story to share that can be tremendously impactful for other people.

In my 25-year career as a coach, trainer, author, speaker, and life-transformer, I've been blessed to coach and impact some of the top pro athletes, executives, and teams in the world. With the tens of thousands of people I've had the opportunity to work with, I've been called a "mindset" coach as much as I have a strength & conditioning coach.

In my time as a trainer and coach, there are some unique quotes I've coined that have since become somewhat "famous":

- "Get your mind right"
- "No more head trash"
- No energy vampires allowed"

- *"Get W.I.T." (Whatever It Takes)*
- *"Find a way"*
- *"And then some"*
- *"Time for IMPACT!!!"*
- And of course, the aforementioned, *"Live a life worth telling a story about…what's your story?!"*

These sayings have helped many people, including myself. Many times, when you are battling through adversity or significant challenge, you create your own mantras, sayings, or affirmations that end up working. And then you use them, and they catch on fire with those you influence. And in this case, it's no different.

With all the men and women I've worked with in my 25-year career, I love to meet people who have the "it" factor. You know, there's just something different about their energy, their presence, or even their massive dreams or big goals. I love that. Or I at least love imparting wisdom and inspiration in someone and seeing if I can ignite a spark that can create an inferno inside of them.

Meet Tim Carter. He's got the "it" factor.

I met Tim on August 7, 2017. I know that date because it's a day I'll never forget. It just so happens that the first NFL athlete I ever worked with, LaDainian Tomlinson, was getting inducted into the Hall of Fame in Canton,

Foreword

Ohio on that day. I was so excited to be in Canton for the ceremonies and to celebrate LaDainian's career after training him for 9-years.

On the morning of one of the most memorable days of my career, I had the opportunity to do a "Hall of Fame Workout & Talk" at my friend Kim Wagler's gym in Canton called Impulse Training. I had known Kim for years because I had the opportunity to work with her in my Mastermind Group as her business coach.

One of the things I most remember about that legendary day and workout was meeting Tim Carter. Tim was a trainer at Impulse Training at the time. He told me he played college football, and he worked at the local college called Walsh University. What I remember most was "the look."

You know, "the look." Not everyone has *it*. But you know it when someone has *it*.

You can tell by the way they move. Or their energy. Or their passion and intensity. Or the way they inspire a group or team. Or a teammate. Or something they say to you and communicate it with honesty, empathy, and conviction.

In Tim Carter's case, it was ALL of this. He clearly had the "it" factor.

About a year later, Tim attended my 3.5 Day Mentorship in San Diego, CA. That was when I really got to know him, and I began to see his passion, desire, and commitment for becoming the best he could be. After that weekend event, Tim joined my Mastermind program and dove in full steam ahead. Since that time, he has been an incredible teammate and has grown immensely in so many ways.

In the Fall of 2023 (just about a year ago as I write this), Tim Carter stood up in front of approximately 100-people at my Annual Retreat for the Mastermind and absolutely stole the show for about 10-minutes. He went on to thank and share extreme gratitude for my entire *Todd Durkin Enterprises* team. He thanked six-people and spoke so eloquently and authentically of what their coaching, mentorship, and guidance has meant over the years. It was one of the most beautiful things I have ever seen.

Tim Carter has a drive and a commitment to excellence that is second-to-none. He is a leader with a strong character, a strong work ethic and a sincere drive to stand out from the crowd. He is also a family-man that is devoted to his wife Riley and his baby girl, Sloane. I love seeing the love he has for his family.

I started this Foreword with the phrase, "Live a Life Worth Telling a Story About, What's Your Story?!" You are soon going to find out in this book that Tim Carter has a remarkable story. In the following pages, he openly shares his challenges and how he climbed out of some of the darkest times of his life. Sometimes in life, we need to breakdown before we can breakthrough. Tim's story epitomizes that.

I also say that "our biggest burdens often become our biggest blessings." That's a sign of *true strength*. Tim Carter's story epitomizes this also. As you read *Find a Way* you will discover not only how this happened for Tim, but more importantly, I think you will see how it can happen for you also.

Throughout the book, Tim gives you action steps to take in order to find your way. His lessons on purpose, being persistent and consistent, doing it anyway, and reaching for the next level are going to show you how to take your current challenge and make it into your own success. I also think you'll enjoy his "Quick Hitters" at the end of the book where he shares motivation and words of wisdom to help you in all facets of your life. Whether you're struggling right now or whether you've overcome some battles and are doing well in life, you are going to get some great wisdom and gems from the lessons Tim shares.

If you are at a point in your life where you need some light, this book will give that to you. The path of life isn't always easy, but as Tim shares in the chapters ahead, you can "find your way."

Peace, love, light, and a ton of impact!

Todd Durkin, MA, CSCS
Founder & CEO, IMPACT-X Performance Fitness & Coaching Franchise
Founder, Fitness Quest 10 & Todd Durkin Enterprises
Head, Under Amour Performance Training Council
2-Time Trainer of the Year (IDEA & ACE)
Top 100 Most Influential People in Health & Fitness
2017 Jack LaLanne Lifetime Award Winner

#GetAfterIt

> **Get After It**—*a slang phrase used to inspire and motivate individuals to seize the day and pursue their goals with determination and enthusiasm.*

It's 3:00 in the morning, and I'm sitting on the gym floor, rolling my feet out, foam rolling my lower and upper body, getting all the weak areas activated. I'm getting ready to put myself through a grueling training session—one that has to be done by 4:42 AM, so I can shower by 4:47 AM, dry off, change and get ready to coach my small group at 5:00 AM.

My eyes are barely open. My mind is racing with over a thousand thoughts—mostly negative, but some positive.

I'm exhausted. My body is aching, my mentality isn't there, and I'm coming up with a list of excuses as to why I should pack it in today.

Time ticks by, and the small window that I have begins to dissipate. Worry and doubt start to creep in from past, triggering moments in my life, which is creating uncertainties about the future. I'm wasting time for no reason thinking about the following:

"Remember when they trusted you and you failed? Over and over again. It will probably happen again"

"Remember the multitude of times you were told you aren't good enough. It's still true"

"Remember what they said about you? They're still saying it. And it's true"

"Remember how bad you were at public speaking and presentations in school? It's still true"

The list goes on.

My pre-workout is finally kicking in, but the motivation to get going is non-existent. In fact, the feeling of doubt and frustration amplifies, and I feel imprisoned by my thoughts and feelings. I am so trapped in head-trash that I am almost to a point where I give up completely. I almost give into the thoughts, worries and fears.

But I didn't.

In fact, what I remember about that moment and other moments is the euphoric feeling that comes after refusing to succumb to those thoughts and fighting through it. I'm talking about the feeling during and after you work out, run, collaborate with good people, read a book that changes your perspective, walk out of church after the pastor's electric message from scripture—you name it.

I say that because it's often the moments before you "start" any of the above experiences that truly test your resolve. When you tap into the resilience on the other side, there is a joy that's created. There is good energy that evolves from it, and a positive affirmation that comes from it.

What I just described to you is a moment that happens more often than you'd think. Maybe not at 3:00 AM anymore, but the moments still happen.

Maybe it happens to you, too, in the morning, afternoon, before bed or even at 3:00 in the morning. Does it happen to you? Of course it does. It happens to everyone.

These are the growth moments in our lives:

- The times we don't feel our best.
- When we let what happened to us in the past affect the here and now.
- The self-doubt that creeps in.
- Doing the things we don't want to do but need to do.

Working through these moments are how we **unlock** our best selves. And to me, it all stems from three words: **Get After It.**

"But wait, Tim. Isn't this book called *Find A Way*?"

You are correct.

But before we get to those three important words, I need you to understand **these three** vital words and what they mean to me.

I told you what the basic definition of "Get After It" was if you were to Google it.

Let me introduce you to mine:

Every day, you have to do something that sucks. Every day.

Challenge yourself to be better. Push past the pain you feel. Do the thing you don't feel like doing.

Trust yourself and who you are, in whatever it is that you do. Lock yourself into that zone where you shut out all the noise, negativity, fear and distractions.

No matter the circumstance, run through it…or get run over by it.

Know that you have the power to be who you want to be, create the life you want to live and get to where you want to go.

Above all else. ***Get after it!***

In other words, do the things that suck. Every day.

Whether you prefer the basic definition or the mantra I just described to you, I want you to understand the third to last sentence of how I described "Get After It."

Know that you have the power to be who you want to be, create the life you want to live and get to where you want to go.

Somewhere in between the power to be who you want to be, the creation of how you want to live and the action that takes you there, there will be many moments you need **breakthroughs** in your life.

Maybe you know this. Maybe you don't. Or maybe you're finding out as you're reading this:

The breakthroughs you want in your life don't come on the days you're motivated.

The breakthroughs come from what you do on the days you don't feel like doing it:

- Getting up early to start the day.
- Getting the sleep and recovery you need to perform at an optimal level.
- Getting your exercise in.
- Eating the right foods and drinking the right fluids that fuel you.
- Reading or listening to good content vs. scrolling social media.
- Your attitude…
- Doing the right thing, even when the right thing isn't easy to do.
- Surrounding yourself with the right people.

On the days that are the hardest, you owe it to yourself to get up, get moving and move the needle. Motivation comes and goes, but discipline and commitment are long-lasting.

Find A Way

Get up. Get After It. Stay after it.

Stop waiting around for things to happen. Time waits for no one, but your best self is waiting for you to make a move.

You already have what you need to move forward… go get better.

The choice is yours…

Find A Way

Since the Fall of 2011, I have worn a wristband with a three-word message: Find A Way.

The year before, "Find A Way" was just a microcosm of words that my high school coach said to our team in the locker room before the Ohio High School Division 3 Football State Championship. At the time, those words had little meaning to me.

As I look back, I'm so fortunate to know that I was a small part of one of the most dynamic and successful teams of all time at Bishop Watterson High School. It was a team that operated and was dialed in on all cylinders. It was a team with an abundance mindset and with coaches, players, equipment and support staff, and athletic trainers from all walks of life, exhibiting their best on any given day, in their specific role. It was a collective group that was *Never Satisfied* and always found ways to get the job done, regardless of circumstance. And it was a family that came together after a 4th quarter, resilient and forthcoming drive from the offense, a slew of consistent, intestinal fortitude from the defense and a routine PAT (point after attempt) that I will forever be grateful for and ultimately led to the hoisting of a championship trophy—the ultimate team win.

Since that Saturday afternoon on December 4, 2010, "Find A Way" developed into something deeper than I could have ever imagined. The following Monday, I continually heard a recording of that same pre-game speech our head coach gave in the locker room, produced by the Columbus Dispatch, the local area newspaper and website. Each time I listened, "Find A Way" in his voice kept getting louder and louder. Clear and concise. Authentic and real. Bone chilling.

The message was clear.

You already know deep down inside of you.

The opportunity is there…so let's go out and make the best of it.

Being resilient and finding a way to get it done.

Keeping your poise when the things in your life do not go your way.

Belief in what you are doing and the person next to you.

Taking on all comers any time and any place. Or rather, facing every situation head on, knowing you have given everything you have.

Go get it done.

Find A Way

We won the Division 3 State Championship that Saturday afternoon because every player and coach on that team was hell bent on finding a way to get it done, regardless of the elements and adversity. Thank you, Coach Dan Bjelac.

More than a decade later, what seemed to be a meaningless three-word message, ultimately became a personal mantra, a divine purpose and a tangible wristband as a reminder.

Let me preface this by saying this book has nothing to do with a football game. It has everything to do with **you.**

But before we go, let me introduce the meaning of those words in my terms.

Find A Way means never being satisfied.

It's the understanding that there is always another level in whatever it is you do.

It's the constant battle of being better than you were the moment before.

It's the pivotal and defining moment where you decide to keep going.

It's getting hit in the mouth and making the unconscious decision to get up, dust yourself off and move forward.

Find A Way

It's the moment that you refute what the devil demands of you and pursue what God has planned for you.

It's the choice you make to reach deeper into the well, even when it seems bare-bones dry.

Find A Way is a message to my younger self and to YOU:

- The things you thought were your weaknesses will ultimately become your strengths through persistence and consistent action.
- The energy and love that's been hidden within you needs to be unleashed in service to others.
- There's another person inside of you that wants it more than you. It's the best version of you. Let that person out.
- Though commitment, the ability to connect with people or conditioning for life might seem unattainable right now, those 3 things can become your divine uniqueness.

What I have for you is not the full story of my life, but profound pieces of it. Each chapter of this book contains a core value, short stories, lessons learned and action items. Though the short story is about my personal experience, the message, lessons and action items are for YOU.

Maybe the story is applicable to you and what you're going through.

Maybe the lessons I learned are some lessons you are about to learn in your own walk of life.

Or maybe, the action items are things that you have been waiting to do and putting off for a long time.

If so, then good. Take this as a sign to go do it.

The ability to be resilient is in all of us. You have the power to create the life you want to live and go where you want to go.

- Take ownership of who you are and what you do.
- Commit to excellence.
- The standard is the standard!
- Live for fulfillment.
- Make someone better.
- Go get what you want out of this life.

Before we become resilient, we need to work through the challenges, barriers and situations that create the breakthrough on the other side.

The physical, mental, or emotional challenges you don't want to face…face them head on anyway.

The barriers that you think are blocking you…break them down anyway.

The uncomfortable situation you're in…get comfortable anyway.

You already know what you need to do. And if you don't, let this be your guide. The choice is yours.

Let's get better.

Find a way.

Chapter 1

Go Deeper

Finding a way requires that we tap into the deepest version of ourselves. There was a time when I was challenged to the point that I had to tap into a deep space inside myself. Let me share that story.

One of the most defining and bone-chilling moments in my life happened on August 7, 2017.

It was Hall of Fame Enshrinement week at the Professional Football Hall of Fame in Canton, Ohio. If you're unfamiliar with Hall of Fame weekend, it is the official time where former NFL greats are inducted and ingrained in history. They are given the most prestigious honor of wearing a gold jacket and forever recognized as legends within the game of football.

Iconic.

The 2017 inductees featured the best of the best. Terrell Davis, Kurt Warner, Jason Taylor, Morten Anderson, Kenny Easley and Dallas Cowboys owner, Jerry Jones.

But, the undisputed leader of that group was LaDainian Tomlinson, one of the greatest running backs of all time.

I remember this because the morning of the enshrinement, I met this guy named Todd Durkin. Todd was Tomlinson's longtime trainer and coach throughout his NFL career, but he was more than just a trainer.

Todd Durkin founded Fitness Quest 10 in San Diego, CA, a world-class training facility in Scripps Ranch. He is a well-renowned strength and conditioning coach, speaker and author with a divine purpose of motivating, educating and inspiring people around the world. He creates **#IMPACT.** (You can read more about him at todddurkin.com)

I share his brief background because as I tell this story, I want you to be in tune to the word in bold—**IMPACT.**

A good friend of mine and former boss, Kim Wagler, owns Impulse Training, which is a private training facility in North Canton, Ohio. Kim and her husband, Chad, have owned Impulse for over 20 years, creating a world-class experience and impacting many lives in that time.

She was a member of Todd's Mastermind group of fitness professionals and gym owners and graciously hosted Todd at her facility for what was known as "Durkin Day."

I was a member at Impulse, and ultimately became a trainer there. I specifically remember Kim talking non-stop for weeks about this "crazy guy named Todd." I had never heard of him until then, but I knew he was a trainer who lived in California and trained professional athletes. He was coming to give a keynote speech at Impulse and to lead a workout in conjunction with a non-profit organization, Hope United, that was represented.

I told Kim all week that I was planning on going, as it was on a Saturday morning before the Hall of Fame festivities kicked off. To me, it seemed like an ordinary Saturday. I might as well go and get a free workout in.

However, it became much more than just an ordinary Saturday. In fact, August 7th, 2017 became a defining moment in my life.

But let me go back a few years to explain where I was and why that day became so important.

For as long as I can remember, I was holding onto a lot of "head trash" in my life. The head trash included harsh feelings, mistakes, emotions and failures I had gone through most of my teenage years, in college and even a few years after. I lacked confidence, whether it was my ability to perform as an athlete, in any public speaking capacity, in my own decision-making or even in my relationships.

I had difficulty controlling my emotions and feelings. If one minor thing went wrong, it affected me ten-fold, and it became a domino effect. A mistake or failure in school, as an athlete or in any social environment seemed like the end of the world to me. I worried constantly about what other people thought of me, wanting to be liked by everyone all the time and feeling mentally paralyzed by any set of adversity that came my way.

Anxiety was eating me alive, and the best way for me to deal with it and suppress it was with alcohol and working out. These two things became coping mechanisms for me, specifically during my junior season at Walsh University.

While choosing the fitness path as a coping mechanism seems like a healthy and logical choice, I chose it in the wrong way.

What's the wrong way?

- Intense workouts and training sessions, two or even three times per day, at a ridiculous level of intensity.
- Not taking days off or allocating time to stretch and recover.
- Measuring the success of each session, lift or run based on how high my heart rate elevated, the number of calories I burned or if I felt breathless by the end.

To me, my training regimen and plan would "balance out" and cleanse the alcohol toxins in my system.

Good strategy, right? Never.

So, my thought was, if I trained hard enough every day, no harm would be done.

To add context, I drank the night before every home game we had. Some nights more so than others. And no one ever knew about. Not my teammates, coaches, or even my parents…which I will never be proud of. It was just my way of getting through it.

It was my way of getting through the season in which I struggled mightily and failed often. It was also my way of getting through the school year, which produced my worst academic performance yet. I was going through the motions in my relationships and friendships, and I was getting worse, day by day and week by week. In fact, it continued through my senior year of college, and it wasn't until after my college graduation that I recognized how bad my mental space was. I even walked across the stage to receive my diploma, sweating profusely through my black cap and gown on a 90 degree day. I was sweating out a 14 day drinking bender I was on as a way to "celebrate". I joked about it with my friends and peers, but truth be told, it tore me up inside.

I was broken.

The fitness and alcohol pattern continued a couple years after college, into my professional and coaching career and even the beginning of graduate school. The best part about that 3-4 year span? No one ever knew about it, recognized it or called me out for it. I hid that aspect of my life well enough for peers, colleagues, players I coached and mentors to never see it. In fact, I was considered by peers and mentors as someone with the following character traits:

- Always had it together and always knew what to say
- The most sensible of the group, always knowing the right thing to do
- Flexible in my approach, relentless in effort and understanding
- "A natural"
- High energy, all the time, with no off button.
- Compassionate

But the truth is, I was burnt out. I was exhausted and lost in what I wanted to do with my life. I was doing so many things all at once at a young age, thinking that I always had to be working, staying busy and productive, working out and training at an insane pace, everything.

I was working full-time as an admissions counselor at Walsh University, volunteering full-time as an assistant coach in the football program, working on my master's degree, helping with a non-profit organization, training clients and former teammates on the side. By my count, I was working 19 hours a day, every day, and only getting 2-3 hours of sleep. Sometimes not sleeping at all.

Go Deeper

Yeah, not good.

You would've never known how tired I was, how empty I felt or the purpose I lacked. Every day I heard from co-workers, teammates, colleagues, and the players I coached: "Man, how are you this energized all the time? You seem like you're always motivated and energetic, ready to take on the next thing."

I heard that statement or some version of it every single day. And I can count a handful of times that I almost snapped and lost it completely. I didn't, though, and I kept moving forward, no matter how difficult it was.

The lone bright spot was dating this incredible woman named Riley, who is now my wife and the mother of our first born, Sloane. Riley is the sole reason I got up that Saturday morning and met Todd Durkin. It would have been much easier to stay in bed because I was really hungover, while alcohol continued its interesting role in my life.

If you thought my drinking before games was bad, in the 2-3 year span after college, I was drinking every weekend, often 1 or 2 days during the week in that three year span. I didn't think anything of it because I was always working out and training, feeling I was in the best shape of my life physically and mentally.

But I was wrong.

The Friday night before Todd's event, I drank…a lot. You name it, I drank it.

Waking up Saturday I felt ashamed and irritable. None of those things aligned with who I was, and I was sulking about it. It was a weird wake up call for me.

I could've stayed in bed that morning, but Riley got my ass (literally) out of bed and told me to go to "Durkin Day."

Thank God for Riley.

On the short, 10 minute drive to Impulse, I reflected on a lot of things that were currently going on in my life and how unhappy I felt. And I cried, uncontrollably. It got so out of hand that I almost veered off the road a few times. I cried because I was so confused on how I could be so unhappy when I had a great job, was in a great relationship, was surrounded by good people and in great physical health.

Do you ever feel that way?

That's the devil working overtime.

- Telling you you're broken.
- Making you feel meaningless and without self-worth.
- Proclaiming you are no one and you have no one.

I looked awful pulling into the parking lot. Dried tears, reeking of alcohol, everything. It's laughable to think about it now.

Go Deeper

I showed up 2 minutes before the event started and walked in the front door. Immediately, I acted like everything was great, regardless of the mess that was going on inside.

Kim saw me right when I walked in and, without any hesitation, gave me a hug and said, "I'm so happy you made it. You're going to love this."

I nodded and smiled like I normally did to put up a facade.

Then, I noticed an abundance of wristbands that said, "Get UR Mind Right" and a wider one that said "IMPACT." Two different, but profound statements that I didn't know I needed at the time. The wristbands were in two separate baskets on the front desk counter. It felt like the wristbands were searing their message into my soul.

Another voice, about five octaves deeper, said, "Those would look great with that Find A Way wristband you have on. Love that mantra."

The voice was Todd Durkin's. *"Nice to meet you,"* he continued. *"You ready to **get after it** today?*

I nodded, still trying to gather my wits around me.

"Good. Let's go."

Sometimes we need validation in our lives to get us back in the saddle. Whether it's the words you're speaking to yourself, a conversation you have with a peer or, quite frankly, a psychological kick in the ass. Over the next two hours, I received all three…and then some.

That day I listened to the best keynote speech I've ever listened to and participated in the most electric workout.

I can still hear the words Todd opened the keynote with:

"Live a live worth telling a story about…what's your story? There's a burning desire in each of your souls and hearts. A desire and pursuit to go deeper on your purpose and who you are, in all that you do. So, my question to you is this…what's stopping you? Is it fear or doubt? Worry or despair? Let it go…let it all go. Today we get better. Today, YOU get better. You owe it to yourself. Go out and create IMPACT in a world that desperately needs it. A world that needs YOU."

The workout we did was **bone-chilling**, but it was exactly what my mind and body needed. It included one hour of high intensity and focused work, plyometric jumps in all planes of motion, TRX movements, sprints, pushups, core conditioning and so much more. It was so intense that I sweated through three shirts and almost puked halfway through. It was a literal cleanse in the purest way.

But the most defining moment that, to this day, altered the course of my life was what Todd said to me during the workout while I was doing band resisted jumps.

Go Deeper

Let me preface this by saying at Impulse, I was known as the "crazy kid", in a good way, of course. I was always amping up an exercise or movement to the next level, challenging myself to be faster, stronger, jump higher, be more explosive, etc. I didn't do it out of ego, but out of sheer intensity and relentless pursuit. Most of the intensity was powered by previous shortcomings, failures from my athletic career, past relationships and people who were in my life.

When I worked out, triggering moments would pop in my head from time to time, and I couldn't let them go. I channeled all of those emotions through fitness and my training routine. I'd train twice a day and sometimes get a third session in, totally disregarding the coaching and advice I'd give to my clients and other people about rest and recovery, listening to your body and allowing yourself grace.

I was in my own head. A lot.

No one knew about it except for me, as we all become experts at hiding our true feelings and emotions. I call it "the mental circle of hell."

But on that day, working out with Todd, something changed.

Mid jump, Todd turned off his headset, put his hand on my shoulder and looked me directly in the eye:

*I got you brother. Let it all out. I get it, and I feel you. I need you to pull that other person out of you and go **DEEPER**! Keep getting after it. **Find a way**.*

Every word he said, I felt immediately in my soul, my bones, everything. This guy I knew for all of 15 minutes just unleashed a caged dog. Literally. I jumped higher, moved quicker and more purposefully. It was a superhuman and euphoric feeling—about 100x that of a "runner's high."

That moment and the remainder of that morning felt like a twilight zone of only good things. Anything bad that happened to me before that no longer existed or mattered. The physical, mental, and emotional pain I had felt for so long subsided.

If you've had that euphoric moment or feeling, you know. And you attempt to hold on to that feeling as long as you can.

To this day, I thank God for that moment.

Every time I see or talk with Todd, I thank him. I thank him for what he said, the look he gave me directly in my eyes that still reverberates in my soul and for being there that day. I thank him for his authentic self and for knowing exactly what I needed to hear and feel that day. That's what the best coaches do.

Todd was just some energetic and crazy trainer I met on a Saturday morning almost seven years ago. Today he

Go Deeper

is my coach, mentor, one of the best people I know, and quite frankly, the guy who saved my life. He's motivated me to live a life worth telling a story about.

Thank you, Todd. For getting my mind right and for the #IMPACT you've had on my life. Because of you, going deeper in my life, health, relationships and career have created profound meaning.

—∞—

Now that you've heard that story, I need you to go deep on yours.

Too often in our lives, we keep everything that hurts us bottled up inside, waiting impatiently to be let go and released.

- The fears, emotions, and doubts that we don't know how to address or fix.
- The bad thoughts and painful memories that overload our minds and hearts.
- The uncomfortable and demeaning conversations that leave a bad taste in our mouths and souls.
- The lies we tell ourselves and the worries that consume our minds.

I hear you. I feel you. I get it. I know.

Honor what you're feeling and then let it go. Even if it's just one thing.

Find A Way

Before you can establish the deepest version of yourself, you need to:

- Surround yourself with the people who challenge you to be at your best. The ones who **unlock** the deepest version of you.
- Take ownership of who you are and what you do. OWN IT.
- Let go of what no longer serves you. Your failures, shortcomings, weaknesses, fears, or past relationships. Let it all go.
- Harness your energy into the good things in your life. The stuff that makes you happy. Get rid of the opposite.
- Maximize the time with the people, places and things that mean the most to you. Time is our most important asset. We don't have enough of it.
- Tell the people in your life you love them. Say what you need to say.

The list goes on. The choice is yours.

Find a way!

Go Deeper

Take Action:

Truth be told, that was a hard story to open up about publicly, as not many have ever heard that.

But I hope that you gained something, even if it's one thing from my vulnerability and honesty.

My action items for you:
- Tell the people who you are close to in your life you love them. Do it, right now.
- Tell your story. No. You don't have to write a book, blog or an article. Start with being open and authentic to the people you surround yourself with. Whether it be family, friends, co-workers, teammates, etc. You never know who your story can help.

Be authentic. Be real. Be forthcoming.

Go make someone better today and every day.

Find A Way!

Chapter 2

Iron Sharpens Iron

One of my favorite verses in the Bible resides in Proverbs 27:17.

"As iron sharpens iron, so one person sharpens another."

Before you can unlock your best self, you need to surround yourself with people who challenge you to be better. The people who sharpen you. The ones who tell you what you need to hear. The ones who have the awareness to challenge you to go to a deeper level. Are you making the conscious choice to better your surroundings and environment? Who are you surrounding yourself with? Are you making someone better?

I want to share a story that is a true pillar of what "Iron Sharpens Iron" means to me. As you read this, I want you to think of all the people in your life who make you better and the reasons why they make you better. Honestly assess who is getting better because of you. Then, I want you to identify how you can get better, so that you can make other people better.

If you aren't at your best when serving others, how can others be at their best?

IMPACT

For the past 10 years, coaching, training and connecting with people has been one of the many blessings in my life. I've had the privilege and fortune of coaching and training a gold mine of good people stemming from youth, high school, college and professional athletes to the general clientele, business owners, medical professionals, weekend warriors, parents, and even the geriatric population. People from all walks of life. I've developed so many great, long-standing relationships in that time and hold many in high regard.

Though I have an abundance of stories and great moments in that time frame, I want to share a profound one, specifically relating to "Iron Sharpens Iron." Angela Hissner is a mother, wife, certified nurse practitioner, avid runner, and one of the best human beings I know. While I was a trainer and coach at Impulse Training, Angela became a member in 2019, and I specifically remember her distinct energy when she came to my bootcamp classes, small group sessions or any session held by all trainers.

Her energy was unmatched, and she always brought the best out of other members and our training staff.

Do you have someone in your life who brings energy and makes you better? Yeah. That was, and still is, Ang Hissner.

At the end of 2019, Angela started doing personal training with me in the mornings and evenings. These were sessions I always looked forward to because I knew she was always working to **get better.** More importantly, I knew she was coachable, had a great attitude and always showed up, no matter what was going on in her life.

Every session was different, but I always had the focus to help her be stronger, more explosive, improve her foundation, balance and core strength and keep her in-tune with her mind and body. But it wasn't because I had the perfect programs or coaching cues. **She** did the work, consistently and persistently, and she deserves all the credit for her results. I was just appreciative of her diligence, and I wanted to make her better. Every day. I could tell you for days about all of the legendary sessions, physical and mental breakthroughs she had, but that's not the point of this.

At the end of 2020, Angela was pressed with a life-altering decision. Her father was in desperate need of a kidney transplant, and it needed to get done as soon as possible. It's a daunting process physically, mentally, emotionally, and spiritually. It's one that can take long periods of time, in more ways than one. Little did her father know, his daughter was going to be the one to step up and donate her kidney.

Though she was nervous, unknowing and anxious about what the consequences would be for her health after the procedure, she knew that it was what was best. I remember this because we talked often about it before, during and after our sessions. I could tell the decision to do it was weighing on her. But she also knew that there was no one better suited to do it than her.

Angela Hissner is an embodiment of Iron Sharpens Iron, in the purest and deepest way. There is no better example than choosing to help her father in a deep, dark time. As her coach and trainer, I was proud and wanted to get her ready as best I could to take this next challenge in her life head on. Some of my favorite training moments stemmed from those last few months before her procedure. All of those moments were based on conversation, telling each other stories and diving deep into life. Those moments made me appreciate my mission as a coach: **Show up and make someone better.** So much so that, the morning of her surgery, I sent her a "pep talk" video while I was mid-workout. It wasn't a plan I had in mind, but it felt like the right thing to do.

Ang Hissner. Wake it up...3:30 AM..Game Day. Just letting you know I'm thinking of you today, especially during kickoff at 7:30 AM…Just keep fighting. Every day, we have to do something that sucks, every single day. Challenge yourself to keep being you and to keep getting better. Can't wait for you and your dad to come out even stronger from this transplant. Always remember to keep that head and heart connection and to keep going, by any means necessary. Love ya, Ang, proud of you. Let's Go!

Do you ever re-watch a video or recording of you talking and you feel awkward or weird? Yes, that was how I felt immediately after sending. Regardless of how it sounded or the sweat and spit that covered my phone after, I know I did my best to help her. All I thought of in that short, one minute video was how could I continue to support her through this challenge in her life and be there as her friend? How could I sharpen her?

Oddly enough, it was her who sharpened me, which is something I realized two months later.

—⚊—

April 2021 was a big transition time in my life. Riley and I were getting married that month and I ultimately made a career transition within the fitness industry. I was leaving Impulse Training and stepping into a new coaching and training role at Cleveland Clinic Akron General. April 22, 2021 was my last day at Impulse and the last sessions I would coach, specifically ending with my final bootcamp in the evening.

For almost 5 years, so much, if not all, of my energy went into coaching, training and connecting with everyone there, whether it was our team, clients or people we'd meet in the community. How fortunate I was to be on a team of people who I consider family and to impact an unbelievable community over that time. I have a lot of love for that place and period in my life. And how fulfilling it was to coach a packed house of some amazing souls, one last time.

It became even more fulfilling when I saw Angela Hissner, one month removed from a kidney transplant, walk through the door. This woman was doing squat jumps, pushups, KB swings, all of it. It was incredible to see, and it lit me up.

After class, I had a great conversation with her on how she was feeling physically and mentally. We connected on all things, including our friendship, past training moments and what the future looked like. Angela and her father were on a challenging road to recovery, but one that I believe they will cherish forever.

One of the best parts? She told me she signed up for the Akron Marathon in September. 6 months after undergoing a kidney transplant. Incredible.

What I thought was an impactful moment became even more impactful later that evening.

Never underestimate the power of a hand-written note and the level of IMPACT it can have.

As I was cleaning up and leaving, we hugged, high fived and fist bumped, and she handed me a card.

I read it the following morning:

"Dear Tim. Can't say thank you enough for all you have done for me. You've made me stronger than I've ever been, have been a constant motivator and pushed me past my limits, but most importantly, you've been my friend. I've never had someone push me and cheer me on the way that you have. You have impacted my life, and I am so thankful to know you. The morning of my surgery, at 3:30 AM, when I was sitting in the hospital staring at the wall starting to freak out, I get a text from you, running on a treadmill giving the best pep talk I've ever had. It was exactly what I needed at the moment, and I will never forget it. You go above and beyond for the people in your life, and it doesn't go unnoticed. I consider you a dear friend and wish you all the happiness in life. Love, Ang"

To this day, I have that letter saved in my desk as a reminder that, everything we say and do for people matters. Be intentional with your words, purposeful in your actions and serve the greater good, for others.

Thank you, Ang, for the letter. I read it often, but most importantly, for the life-long friendship and memories we created. Thank you for sharpening me.

Iron sharpens iron isn't just a Bible verse or inspirational quote. It's what we're called to do in this life. Every day.

An exercise I've done consistently for several years is called 10 Forms of Wealth, made famous by Wayne Cotton and introduced to me by the Todd Durkin Mastermind. Every month I do this exercise and rank 1-10 on where I am at in my own forms of wealth.

10 Forms of Wealth

1. Spiritual/Inner Self
2. Physical
3. Mindset
4. Family
5. Professional
6. Financial
7. **Circle of Genius/Social**
8. Adventure
9. Love
10. IMPACT/LEGACY

I want to touch on the Circle of Genius aspect.

The Circle of Genius takes a step deeper and helps you identify:

1. Who's sharpening you and who **should** be sharpening you?
2. Who are you sharpening and who **should** you be sharpening?

Notice the difference between the first and second clause in those two prompts.

Who's sharpening you and who should be sharpening you?

This is pretty simple.

Who are you hanging out with? Who are you training with? Who's filling up your cup? Are you around people, co-workers, teammates, and family that make you better or worse?

I'll give you an easy answer on who and what you **shouldn't** be around:

- Energy vampires – what they say is true and they will suck the energy out of you
- Complaining and whining
- Gossip
- Mr. and Mrs. Excuse- the ones who have an excuse for everything!
- Overly pessimistic people – being realistic is one thing, but do you really want to be around someone who sees the negative all the time?

Who are you sharpening and who should you be sharpening?

Another simple one. What does leading by example mean to you? We are under a microscope every day, every moment and every hour. Iron sharpens iron is about first being self-honest and showing integrity. Is the tool you are using actually sharpening the intended person?

What words or message are you speaking to others on a daily basis?

What actions are you carrying out?

Everything we say and do matters, whether we realize it or not. The undeniable truth is that we are all in a position to make people better, regardless of your occupation or role.

- Help the student understand the lesson plan
- Give your client, customer or patient undivided attention
- Hold your significant other's hand
- Play outside with your kids
- Be a great teammate
- Send the encouraging text, phone call or email
- Tell the people in your life you love them.

In some way, shape or form, we are called to make someone better.

Get up. Show up. Get Better. Make someone better.

Find A Way!

Take Action:

Once we fully understand the meaning of Iron Sharpens Iron, we need to put it into practice, every day.

On a personal level, my challenge to you is this. I want you to take a snippet from the Circle of Genius form of wealth:

1. Write down 3-5 important people in your life. It can be family, spouse, friends, co-workers, etc. Then, I want you to write one bullet point on how you can make each of those 3-5 people better TODAY. Remember, Iron Sharpens Iron is a DO NOW action item
2. Write down 3-5 people or groups that you're currently surround yourself with. Then, ask the question if you are truly getting better from each person/environment. If you can't answer the question immediately, maybe it's time to be around different people? Maybe it's time to join a mastermind group, church group OR just find people that make you BETTER.

Be intentional. Be purposeful. Go get better!

Chapter 3

Purpose

Purpose given. Mission driven.

Before we can unlock our best selves, we need to find our purpose, then utilize it to serve a deeper calling.

Kelli Watson is one of the Platinum Level Coaches in the Todd Durkin Mastermind group which I have been a part of since November of 2019. The TD Mastermind is a gold mine of good people, fitness professionals, gym owners, coaches, and trainers who all have a desire to level up their personal and professional lives. We dive deep into consistently evolving in all aspects of business, marketing, strategic planning and life. But the true fulfillment I have found in the group lies in the relationships and friendships I've built and the long-standing impact we are committed to leaving, together.

Let's call it "Iron Sharpens Iron," which is what you read about previously.

Kelli Watson is a wife, mother, coach, author, business owner, and a divinely unique person. She is a constant reminder of who I am and what I am meant to do. Above all else, she challenges me to be better in all areas. She is the epitome of **Find A Way.**

Everyone needs a Kelli Watson in their lives.

I met Kelli in November of 2019 at one of Todd's 3.5 Day Mentorship programs at Torrey Pines in La Jolla, CA. These mentorship retreats present the opportunity of growing personally, professionally, and even spiritually. This specific retreat had nearly 75+ fitness professionals and high-level business owners in the room.

Let me preface this by saying the trajectory of my life changed when I met Todd Durkin in 2017, but my vision was truly refined just by attending this 3-day retreat and being in the room full of purposeful people.

As I write this, I know that God put Kelli Watson in my life for a reason, which is one that I will never forget. Kelli and I had a 3-minute conversation on the first day, before the retreat even started. I specify that the conversation was 3 minutes on **purpose**. I introduced myself, told her what I do, where I am from, and why I am here.

The following evening, Todd graciously hosted all attendees at this home to appropriately close what had been an amazing weekend. Though the experience and vacation were great, I felt there was something more that I needed before flying back to Ohio the next day. I sat around a fire in Todd's backyard and Kelli happened to be directly across from me. At the time it seemed *coincidental*, but now I know it was what I needed.

"A coincidence is a miracle in which God chooses to remain anonymous."

We talked about our lives and families, how great the weekend was, the usual small talk. Then, as I felt called to do so, told Kelli that I had no idea what my purpose was. I told her I was struggling heavily in what it was that I was being called to do and the direction I was headed. That I needed to be at this mentorship retreat. I needed help.

Kelli smiled, looked me directly in the eye and said this:

"Tim Carter. Your purpose is your ability to move someone's current energy to another level. It is your commitment and investment in caring for somebody and making an impact. You see the good in other people and it moves you to create that experience. Your energy, passion, and ability to elevate others is what you're meant to do."

God things.

There are unbelievable moments and then there are WOW moments that introduce yourself to who you really are. It took me 26 years to recognize what my purpose was. For Kelli, it took 3 minutes on the first day of meeting me. It took her only 3 minutes because she recognized the conviction in my voice, gave me undivided attention and made a connection with me.

I remember every word she said to me that evening in November of 2019. I remember it because it was the third time in my life that someone saw something in me that I did not realize before. The first time was my beautiful wife, Riley. The second time was Todd Durkin.

A 3-minute conversation connected to a 3-word phrase, **Find A Way.**

In the 4+ years I have known Kelli, she has challenged me to be better, deeply cared for me personally and professionally, and has always been authentic with me. In a full circle moment, as a co-owner of Scriptor Publishing Group, she has spearheaded the effort in releasing this book to you. Most importantly, she has reminded me and many others of a distinct lesson:

Everything we do starts with your foundation and who we are at home.

Yes, we want to improve our business, move the needle in our careers, grow our network, be a better athlete or student, and make more money. However, we need to be great within ourselves and at home first.

- Be a great significant other.
- Be a great parent or grandparent, uncle or aunt, brother or sister, son or daughter, niece or nephew.
- Be a great listener and connect deeply.

Purpose

- Be a diligent worker and commit to the ordinary and extraordinary tasks.
- Be great in your health and wellness journey.
- Be great at being who YOU are. No one else.

The list goes on. Finding your *purpose* requires you to be great at home first.

Your purpose is the foundation and core of all that you do.

For me, there is conviction in raising someone's energy to a different level. There is undivided attention to caring for somebody and making an impact, whoever it is that God puts in front of me. There's an undeniable connection when you see the good in other people and commit to delivering a great experience.

Energy, tenacity, and commitment to caring define my purpose.

Thank you, Kelli Watson, for reminding me who I am and what I am meant to do in this life. Your thoughts, words and actions have propelled me forward. Most importantly, you have been a godsend in my life as my coach, mentor, and friend.

Everyone needs a Kelli Watson in their lives. They might be the person that helps you find your purpose and refine your vision.

Do you have yours?

Take Action:

In the introduction I mentioned a few things that went from weaknesses to strength for me:

A. Commitment to who you are and what you do
B. Ability to connect
C. Conditioning for life – physical, mental, emotional, intellectual, and spiritual

Those 3 strengths stemmed from my personal core values. So, my action item for you is to write or type your core values, as they relate to who you are as a person. Need help finding those? Use the letters in your name! I'll share mine:

Tenacity, **I**ntegrity, **M**otivating, **C**ompassionate, **A**mbitious, **R**esilient, **T**rustworthy, **E**nergizing, **R**espect

Before you can find and establish your purpose, start with the small details that define who you are and go deep on each of them.

1. Write down your core values and then start living them out. Everything we do starts with our foundation and core of who we are.
2. Share them! Your gifts, purpose and core values are meant to spread the good and impact other people. Share them in person, on social media, in your journal, or even with me!

I need you at your best and the world needs you at your best.

Find A Way!

Chapter 4

Be Persistent to be Consistent

The best way to find consistency is to be consistent.

Read that again.

A favorite book of mine is *212 Degrees, The Extra Degree* by Sam Parker and Mac Anderson. At 211 degrees water is hot. At 212 degrees water comes to a boil. Boil produces steam. And the steam is that extra facet that can power a locomotive. It's the continual application of heat to every task. Every day.

If you are doing the math, all that it took to power the locomotive was 1 degree.

Whether it's 1 degree, 1 percent, 1 step or 1 inch, it is a reminder to all of us that we need to strive to make progress every day. Seek continual improvement and focus on the areas of your life that you MUST be better in:

- Your personal health
- Your relationships

- Your business or career
- Your attitude
- Your finances

The list goes on, but there's a deeper level to the 212 degrees story. The deeper level is your commitment and consistency to personal habits. Do you have someone holding you accountable to those?

"If your habits are dialed in and consistent, you get better. If your habits suck and are inconsistent, you get worse. Make sense? Good. Do better."

The above quote is what Frank Pucher told me on a call I had with him in March of 2021.

> Frank Pucher is a business coach, presenter and award-winning fitness entrepreneur. He is a Platinum Level Coach & The Director of the Todd Durkin Mastermind Program which serves fitness entrepreneurs from around the country. Frank is the former CEO of Fitness 121 Personal Training. He developed and ran that business in Roseland, NJ for 20 years from 1998-2018. During the time Frank owned Fitness 121, it was twice named New Jersey's "Best Personal Training Studio."
>
> In 2018, Frank published his book, *Smart Money Moves: The Fitness Professional's Guide for Earning, Growing and Protecting Your Money*, which became an Amazon Best Seller.

Frank is the Director of the Todd Durkin Mastermind, one of the Platinum Level Coaches, a former business owner, author, and dedicated athlete, among many other things. Like Kelli, Frank is a coach, mentor, and friend that I am grateful for and truly appreciate.

Ego aside, let me divulge into everything that was going on in my life in March of 2021

- Riley and I just moved into and were working on our severely unfinished home, which will be another story later.
- We were preparing like mad for our wedding in April
- I was working two jobs. 1 full-time within higher education and 1 as a trainer and coach, in what sometimes felt like 20 hours a day.
- I was waking up at 2:15 AM and going to bed at 10 PM (sometimes not going to bed at all). Every day. Like clockwork.
- I was training for 2 Ironman70.3 races that summer.

Sometimes we drink a glass of water and other times we are drinking from a firehose. I was drinking from a firehouse.

Does this sound like what you are going through right now or have gone through previously? Good, keep reading.

Every two to three months, I schedule a call with Frank to go over the next 90 days, plan out the following quarter, set challenging and attainable goals, and hone in on what he calls the "Core 4":

- Health
- Wealth
- Relationships
- Experience

The Core 4 is meant to **simplify** the items and goals we need to take action on. These 4 aspects are the foundation of our lives and where we can measure what success and fulfillment look like.

1. Where are you at physically, mentally, emotionally, and spiritually in your overall **health** and wellness? What areas can you improve upon.
2. How are you defining what **wealth** looks like to you? Is it solely a measure of your financial state or is there a deeper meaning to you?
3. How are your **relationships** with your significant other, immediate and extended family, your team, co-workers and inner circle?
4. What **experiences** are you most looking forward to and how often do you want to create experiences? Do you need a vacation, time off or time in solitude? What do you NEED to experience now?

The Core 4 is about what makes the most sense to you and identifying the actions you need to take to improve among all 4 areas. The actions and habits that need to take place every day, **consistently**. The Core 4 keeps me grounded and in this particular call, was a psychological kick in the ass. One that taught me a valuable lesson in focus, preparation, and execution on the small details.

In the beginning of the call, Frank asked what had and had not been working well in the Core 4. Without even listening to the question, I told him everything that was going on in the current month and rest of the year, the bullet points you read above. That's when he caught me.

When you see Frank smile and perk up on a Zoom call or while you are talking to him in person, 100% of the time, you are going to get hit with undeniable, harsh truth. I've been doing these calls **consistently** with Frank since the end of 2019. I schedule and block out this time to connect with him because he makes me better. His coaching and guidance have made me a better husband, father, coach, trainer, and human being. I value the time working and learning from him because he listens first, asks me the tough questions, and tells me what I **need** to hear, not want. That is what great coaches do.

I remember what he told me next because it will always be applicable to everything that we do.

"Tim. Sounds like you have a lot going on, and I am proud of you. But let's step aside on this as I want to tell you a profound, but simple story. It's called the Aggregation of Marginal Gains."

The Aggregation of Marginal Gains is a parable that details the **consistent** actions of the British Cycling Team. If you've read *Atomic Habits* by James Clear, you may have heard this story.

The British Cycling Team overcame nearly 100 years of mediocrity and has since become the most dominant cycling team of all time, detailing the last 15 years. They have won a multitude of World Championships, gold medals in the Olympic & Paralympic Games and have dominated the Tour de France. Most would look at the macro of their accomplishments, but Frank wanted me to focus on the micro details that led to those feats.

Similar to the 212 degrees story, the team committed to the continual application of good habits they formed from their coach, Dave Brailsford. Dave's philosophy was to start from the foundation and core of each individual and make the necessary improvements in all the details that were required for a cyclist to become the best version of themselves. This concept is something we hear often, the 1% better approach. Before we can establish consistency, we need to consistently take action on the habits that make us 1% better and 1 degree better. We need to progress.

For the British cycling team, the consistent action and progressing on good habits repeatedly, added up to a World Class cycling team.

And, if a simple concept can help a cycling team win multiple sporting events, it can help improve your life.

What I realized after that call was that I was too focused on the end results and forgot about the process. The end results are great, but the persistence of focusing on the process is what makes us better.

Frank gave me a reminder that day to focus on improving one thing and then to keep improving it by consistent action. Though I had many things on my mind in March of 2021, he got me refocused on the task at hand and locked in on what was right in front of me. "Do Better" as he would call it.

Trust the process and you will make progress day after day and moment to moment.

Because you are wondering about the end results of March 2021 bullet points:

- Today we are grateful to live and experience our beautiful home. Though each day and project in our house was different, we stayed diligent in the process of creating and defining what "home" looked like to us. (And we continue to do so, everyday)
- Our marriage continues to get stronger day by day, month by month and year by year because we are dedicated to the process of growing our

relationship. We show up for each other and do the work, every day.
- I am fulfilled in my career journey in what I am doing as a coach, professional, speaker and now author because I was focused on consistently improving each area, one thing at a time.
- Consistent sleep is a work in progress, but it is a process I am willing to work through.
- My performance in both IM70.3 races qualified me for All World Status that year. But the focus on getting better remains. And I continue to get better by showing up, doing the work and being consistent.

Thank you, Frank, for being authentic and real, asking the tough questions and telling me what I need to hear. It is your diligence, commitment to #DoBetter and your unwavering consistency that has made me 1% and 1 degree better, every day.

So how is this applicable to you? Maybe you are experiencing the following:

- You are stuck in finding a good routine.
- You are struggling to figure out what's next in your life.
- Your habits suck and you need to find better ones.
- You are worried or too focused on the end result that you forget the details to get there.
- You need someone to hold you accountable.

Be Persistent to be Consistent

Maybe it is something else, but the profound, raw and authentic message stays the same:

- Improvement and progress are best measured by being 1% or 1 degree better, every day.
- Stop talking about what you are going to do. Words dissipate in the air, actions are long lasting. Be about it and do it consistently.
- Good habits move the needle. Bad habits remove the needle. Get rid of your bad habits, now.
- Stop worrying about the sexy stuff and keep doing the mundane tasks over and over again. Perfect the details. Then move on. #Frankism
- Do the things you do not want to do, then do them again, regardless of how hard it is or how much it sucks. F****** do it.
- Show up every day as who you are and then do the work.

It's your life. You are responsible for your results. Take ownership in what you do. Attack every task with a purpose. Commit to excellence in what you do. Get up, get moving and go get better.

Consistency is applicable everywhere and in every aspect.

Find a way to be consistent.

Take Action:

In this chapter you heard a couple short stories about 212 degrees and the British Cycling team. Both centered around the concept of being 1% or 1 degree better every day.

Now, I want you to use the Core 4 exercise that Frank introduced to me and come up with 2-3 things in each area that you can improve upon.

1. Health
2. Wealth
3. Relationships
4. Experience

Remember, keep it simple. Bullet points work. Recognize the aspects in each of the 4 that you need to get better at.

There are no wrong answers, just forward movement.

As always, share your action items or your takeaways with me. Together we can hold each other accountable and get better.

Find a way!

Chapter 5

Do it Anyway

Before we can unlock the best version of ourselves, we need to establish authenticity, honing in on what makes us divinely unique. Knowing that regardless of the trials and tribulations, criticism and doubt along the way, showing up as who you are and doing the work you're called to do will win out.

In the last few years, I've found myself coming back to a profound perspective on life, made famous by Mother Teresa.

"Do It Anyway"

People are often unreasonable and self-centered. Forgive them anyway.

If you are kind, people may accuse you of selfish motives. Be kind anyway.

If you are honest, people may cheat you. Be honest anyway.

What you spend years building, someone can destroy overnight. Build anyway.

The good you do today, people will often forget tomorrow. Do good anyway.

If you find happiness, they may be jealous. Be happy anyway.

Give the world the best you have, it may never be enough. Do your best anyway

It's an analysis on life that I use often and was reminded of by a great friend and teammate, Jill Rooks. I met Jill in person in October of 2020 in San Diego at a retreat. She's a Platinum Level Coach in the Todd Durkin Mastermind just like Frank and Kelli.

> Jill, based in Loma Linda, CA, and a business owner in Redlands, CA, embarks on a profound journey driven by her passion for health and well-being. Introduced to fitness in 7th grade by her parents, she later explored swimming and water polo in high school. Jill learned early the vital role of movement for her health, given her family's history of heart disease. Her 30-year weight loss journey deepened her understanding of the intrinsic link between physical and mental health, inspiring her to establish The Energy Lab in 2011, with its complementary yoga-inspired space, The Fort. Rooted in her belief in the interconnectedness of mind, body, and spirit, Jill is committed to facilitating holistic well-being for her clients. Guided by the proverb, "If you want to go fast, go alone. If you want to go far, go together," Jill thrives on collaboration, exemplified by her involvement with Todd Durkin's Mastermind since 2009, leading to her role as a coach within the Mastermind team, where she thrives on supporting fellow fitness professionals and entrepreneurs in their journeys toward success. Her WHY, rooted in her father's passing from a heart attack, drives her mission to promote heart health and holistic wellness.

Jill is an embodiment of how we view service to others, peace, patience, and "doing it anyway."

Oddly enough, before we met in person, I had connected with her online in 2017 on a fitness platform called MyZone, which is a world-class business providing wearable technology that measures precise heart rate tracking and personal effort with real-time feedback. There was a MyZone challenge that ran through the Fall of 2017, featuring 10 gyms across the country. This challenge measured "MEPs" (MyZone effort points) over the course of the 4th quarter. The winner was determined by total MEPs by the end of December.

I was a client at Impulse at the time, working out like crazy with a few other members and coming up with creative ways to earn more MEPs for this challenge. I'd be at it for hours before going to work; running, box jumps, hitting the heavy bag, pushing the sled. You name it, I did it.

***Disclaimer. Don't attempt that level of strenuous exercise just to accumulate points for a challenge.

I even wore my MyZone belt while coaching in practices and games at Walsh. (In fact, I went so hard over that time frame that I got sick and was down for the count for over a week!)

And still, it wasn't enough. Jill's Energy Lab team blew everyone out of the water. They won because of the consistent, collective effort of all who were involved. Knowing when to push the needle, dial it back and recover. They won because they continued doing the hard things, even when they didn't feel like doing them. These people were energizing, constantly moving throughout the day, fun-loving, and a unique group. It was obvious that Jill has built and continues to grow an outstanding community.

Like many successful teams, success and fulfillment start from consummate leadership and making your team better. The leadership that motivates someone to get better, no matter the circumstance or situation. Doing it anyway even when you don't feel like doing it. Not only a statement, but a profound, consistent action. Leader of one and leader of many is a great way to describe Jill Rooks.

There are specific people that God places in your life for dynamic reasons. Sometimes, those people live on the other side of the country. I believe Jill to be one of those divinely unique people.

I've seen Jill in person 5 times in the 4+ years I've known her. Though the visits and retreats are short, 3 day excursions, each experience has been memorable, soul enlightening and reminds me how important it is to be around people that make us better. The most profound connection I have with Jill is how we share perspectives, specifically, inspiration from Mother Teresa's "Do It Anyway" analysis.

In August of 2022, Jill led a coaching call and centered key performance indicators around the concept of "doing it anyway" within our businesses, personally, professionally, and with others around us. It was a beautiful analysis of everyday life.

Some days you won't want to wake up.
Wake up and be you, anyway.

Find A Way

Some days you won't feel like exercising.
   Go to the gym, anyway.

Some days you won't feel like fueling your body.
   Fuel your body, anyway

Some days you won't hit your goal.
   Keep being diligent, anyway.

Some days our clients will be difficult with us.
   Smile and work with them anyway.

Some days will be harder than others.
   Keep doing the work whole-heartedly anyway.

The list went on, but the message is clear.

Doing it anyway requires us to keep doing the hard things, even when we don't want to. It demands our very best, not only in the moments when we feel great, but in the situations and tribulations that take away our peace, patience and fortitude.

It's a mentality first, then an action of continuing to show up on the hard days and face the things you don't want to face. It's controlling the controllables and letting go of the things we cannot. It's the criticism we face, whether it be internally or externally, and making the decision to press on anyway.

There are things in our lives that we don't feel like doing, but we have to get them done to get moving forward. Sometimes they are simple and mundane. Other times they are complex.

- Waking up early to exercise.
- Reading good content vs. scrolling social media.
- Spending time with your kids vs. watching TV
- Eating the foods that fuel and nourish you
- Having the difficult conversation you keep putting off.
- Meeting your deadlines at work.
- Listening before talking.

The list goes on.

On a deeper level, "doing it anyway" is the opportunity to be your authentic self. Knowing there will be criticism, comparison traps, anxiousness, and uncomfortable situations that present themselves.

Being your authentic self and doing it anyway can be boiled down to 2 things, which are deeply connected:

1. Character over criticism
2. Will over worry

Your character is your uniqueness and who you are. Your will is the resilient action you take to continually evolve your character.

You're going to face criticism no matter what you do. Good, bad or indifferent.

Every day of your life.

Find A Way

You could be the most genuine person on the planet, kind to everyone and always in service to others, and you would still be criticized for who you are or what you do. You can't please everyone. You can't be everything to everyone. You can't help people who don't want help. Trust me. I've tried.

But don't let that stop being who you are. Ever.

Let your true character win out, in all situations.

Your habits become your character. Your character becomes your legacy.

Your character is who you are, defined by your thoughts, words, actions and habits.

My character has led me to define myself as a high-energy person, seeking the good in others, showing compassion and working to make others around me better.

For me, not everyone I've come across molds well with high energy people. Some will criticize you for showing great energy.

Not everyone will choose to see the good and positive things in others, some will belittle you for it.

Not everyone will want to show compassion, regardless of circumstance, and will be angry with you for it.

Not everyone wants to make people better, and they will laugh at you for it.

Here's the thing:

Part of the process of unlocking your best is understanding that not everyone will understand your process.

So, here's my version of "Do It Anyway":

Not everyone will be appreciative of the work you do. Keep doing great work, anyway.

Not everyone will be as compassionate to others as you are. Be compassionate, anyway.

Not everyone will see the good in others the way that you do. See the good in others, anyway.

Not everyone has the desire to make people better. Make someone better, anyway.

And finally…

Not everyone will be as on fire as you are. Be on fire, anyway!

You were built different and meant to be different. Own it!

Take Action:

In the first sentence of this chapter, I suggested that it is our authenticity that makes us divinely unique. Who we are and what we do consistently defines our character.

1. In 3-5 words or statements, describe your character in **your** eyes and heart. Remind yourself of your gifts, talents and what you represent.
2. Now that you've written down those 3-5 words or statements that define who you are, proclaim 1 action item for each that you are committed to doing…and then record the result… and then keep doing it.

And if you don't feel like doing the above exercise? **Do it anyway.**

Find A Way!

Chapter 6

Suck It Up

The game of football has been a centerpiece in my life for almost 16 years. So many life lessons for me have come from either playing or coaching during that time frame. One of those distinct life lessons came during a Spring practice of my freshman year at Walsh University.

It was March 2012, the second to last day of Spring Ball, and it was 15 degrees, cold, rainy, and miserable, to put it mildly.

I had strep throat and some other "stuff" that happened that week and the previous two months, lost close to 15 pounds in a few days and wanted nothing to do with anything or anybody.

You ever get in that phase? Yep.

My body language was shit and I was sulking about it. I was in my own head, which, is never a place you want to be. And all of what I mentioned affected my schoolwork, relationships and social life.

To add to that, if you measured the energy level of the other 90 players (and even coaches) on our team, you could tell that no one wanted to be out there. Except for one man, Coach John Fankhauser.

Coach Fank is one of my favorite coaches I've ever had. He was the one who developed a great relationship with my family and me, recruited me to Walsh, challenged me to my absolute core in the time I've known him and always demanded my best as a player and coach.

Fank is an "old-school" guy. He is hard-nosed, mentally and physically tough, blue collar, authentic, and a no bull-shit guy. Plus his forearms are made of bricks. Currently, he is the Head Football Coach at Walsh University, but at the time, he was our Running Back coach, Special Teams coordinator, specialty coach and well-renowned groundskeeper at Walsh. Everyone that knows him has nothing but resounding respect and praise for his work "in the trenches." Not to mention, he was a former fullback at Youngstown State when they won three National Championships under Jim Tressel.

Did I mention hard-nosed? Yeah.

We were in the middle of the dynamic warmup before practice and honestly, I was just going through the motions, coughing, sneezing, and just trying to get through the practice. I felt miserable, unmotivated, lethargic, and my body language accentuated all of that. Fank came over and talked to me, as he usually does to cover what we were doing at practice.

"Tim Carter how we doing this morning? Ready to go?" he asked.

Without much consideration, I told him, "Coach, feeling pretty awful. Have had strep and haven't been able to eat or sleep those last couple days. Just trying to get through." I was making excuses, complaining, all of it. Looking back now, I laugh about how whiny it seemed.

Without hesitation, Fank grabbed my shoulder pad with his left hand and threw a forearm shiver directly to my facemask…and it knocked me square on my ass. He then said, "Tim, my 4 year old daughter has strep throat. Suck it up and let's go." I rolled my eyes, got up and went back to the usual warmup routine.

I remember that moment because it happened three other times during practice that day. Fank could tell my body language sucked, so he purposefully ran into me, threw a few forearms, etc. Looking back on it, I'm sure my teammates were wondering why he was doing it and what purpose it served. It seemed comical and embarrassing on my part. Though it irritated and flustered me at the time, I knew Fank always had a reason behind everything he did. In fact, he told me as we were making the cold walk off the field after practice that day.

"Tim, do you know why I'm so hard on you all the time? Do you know why I was knocking you on your ass today? It's because the Tim Carter I saw in pre-practice was not the Tim Carter I know. It wasn't the guy I recruited, shared personal stories with and the deep young man I got to know. I haven't seen him the last couple days, but I'd love to see him out there again. Because that young man is resilient, cares for others, shows great pride in what he does and is one hell of a leader and teammate.

What I'm trying to tell you is that there's another person deep inside of you that wants it way more than you do. That's the Tim Carter I know and love. I need you to dig and find that person again. By any means necessary. It's time to suck it up and get better. And I know you will."

That was all I needed to hear in the most humbling way possible.

More than a decade later, I still consider it to be one of the best things that ever happened to me. Sure, "suck it up" can be interpreted loosely and in different ways, but Coach Fank knew what to say to me that day and in that moment. I didn't *want*, to hear it, but I **NEEDED** to hear it. And because of that, I remind myself often when I get in those "moods". I needed to get my head back in the game, to stop making excuses, feeling sorry for myself and letting it affect other aspects of my life.

Here's the undeniable truth:

Before we can get to the next level of our lives, we need to suck it up, dig deeper and get better in all aspects.

That practice and the moment after was one of the best things that ever happened to me. And I will truthfully say that Coach Fankhauser is one of my favorite coaches and people in my life.

I say that practice was life altering for three reasons

1. I had a bit of an ego on how "good" I was.
2. It was at a time that I was still understanding what toughness truly was, physically, mentally and emotionally.
3. It was at a time where I would complain and worry about things often without being aware of the effect it had on my performance on the field, in school and out.

As much as it altered my life for the better, it gave me fuel, motivation and a higher standard I held myself to for the rest of my playing career, and my life.

- It made me a better student, athlete and teammate.
- It made me more coachable and a forever student of the game.
- It made me self-aware of my language, both verbal and non-verbal, and exemplified how to lead by example.

- It challenged me to keep getting up, no matter how many times in my career that I failed (and I failed, a lot!)
- It helped me understand another meaning of **Find A Way.**

Because of that moment, I knew I could trust him as a coach, leader, and mentor, knowing he would always be honest and forthcoming, authentic and challenge me to be better. I trusted him as the coach who recruited me, my position coach, mentor, colleague, one of the respectable faces of the University, and most importantly my friend.

Every time I see Coach Fank, I thank him for that day in March of 2012. I thank him because he made me better that day and every day that he's been my coach. He's sharpened who I am as a person, husband, father, coach, student of the game and then some. I'm stronger, more resilient, and aware because of that simple lesson Fank taught me that day.

Sometimes, we have to suck it up and keep moving, regardless of circumstance, trials, or tribulations. Am I still working through physical, mental, and emotional toughness? Absolutely and it continues to be in practice every day.

Are there still times that I complain and worry about things? Absolutely and it continues to be worked on in different ways.

Suck It Up

The point is, we have to keep working through our weaknesses, liabilities and "head trash" before we can achieve the strength we want. And then, we need to literally "suck it up" and keep moving. Even if you're sick, hurt, injured, letting your emotions get the best of you, we need to find ways to keep moving forward.

When you're sick, find ways to get healthier.

When you're hurt or injured, find ways to recover, take care of your mind and body and do the necessary things to relieve pain in the healthiest way possible.

When your emotions get the best of you, honor those emotions. Once you've acknowledged them, now it's time to move forward and let them go.

"Suck it up" isn't just an old adage that's meant to sound demeaning, belittling, or discouraging. It's meant to help us understand that we can always do and be better, by any means necessary, anywhere necessary and for any amount of time necessary.

Thank you, Coach Fankhauser, for always telling me what I need to hear, challenging me to my core, sharpening me, and for the unfiltered reminders to suck it up and get better!

It's no secret that before we can unlock our best selves, we need to be around the people that make us better. The people that make us better are authentic and real, honest and forthcoming, purposeful and diligent. They don't tell you what you want to hear, but what you **need** to hear. What you need are the people with no façade, who are unfiltered and divinely unique. That's how you "suck it up" and get better. By surrounding yourself with coaches, mentors and people that demand your best, regardless if you're feeling your worst.

Those people are the ones who truly care about you and your well-being.

> **Take Action:**
>
> 1. Where in your life right now can you "suck it up" and get better? It's applicable everywhere. At home, work, in the gym, your kitchen, church, everywhere.
>
> Maybe as a parent, leader in your community or teammate?
>
> 2. Choose 1-2 things of your personal life and professionally where you need to suck it up, get in the trenches and **WORK**, write them down and then intentionally do them.

Chapter 7

Locked In

Before we can establish the next level of peace and solitude, we need to work through the noise in our lives. Flipping the switch in your mind that locks you into the task at hand, zoning in on what's right in front of you and leaving nothing to chance.

Unlocking your best self requires a committed level of focus from you in all that you undertake. Focus isn't a talent. It's a defined skill that's worked on consistently, edited and revised and evolves over time.

"But, what if I'm not good at focusing?" is often a question I get from clients, co-workers, family and friends.

Everyone is good at focusing, but maybe it's not on the right things.

To me, focus and solitude are intertwined and can be enhanced in two different aspects:

1. Poise under pressure.

2. Calm within the chaos.

Within each of those aspects is a personal parable or short story on being **locked in**to what's in front of you, the things that matter and operating at your best. Let me preface this by saying it took failure, trials, and tribulations to fully understand what establishing focus and solitude really meant for me.

I say that because, in your own journey, you're going to learn and understand what your next level focus and solitude looks like. It doesn't have to be exactly like mine. Ever. But I want you to visualize your own life and journey within each parable, lesson and action items. What makes the most sense to you?

Whether you're a business owner, teacher, medical professional, coach, parent, athlete or student, it's no secret that peace and solitude are often difficult to maintain, let alone find. But the only way to find it is by doing something about it.

Poise under pressure

It's the final drive in regulation of the Walsh University and Lake Erie College game in October of 2012.

The score is even with our offense driving down the field with a chance to win in the final seconds. I'm getting one final kick into the net on the sideline as it's now 3rd down inside the 20 yard line with under a minute to go.

Locked In

I jog down the sideline, standing next to Coach Fank, before head coach, Jim Dennison, makes the call for the field goal team.

I'm shaking.

I had just missed an extra point on the previous touchdown drive and a field goal earlier in the first half. But I had a third chance at redemption and putting all of that behind me. Just two years before, I was one of the most reliable kickers and punters in the state of Ohio on the 2010 State Championship team at Bishop Watterson High School I rarely missed, and I was known for delivering in the clutch by never letting anything take away my confidence or letting distractions get in my way.

I was solid. I was locked in mentally and physically, until that Sophomore season in college. My preparation during the off-season, summer and in-season was always intentional, purposeful, and solidified. My confidence, mental dexterity, and belief in my abilities were there.

But something happened that Fall that completely destroyed my confidence in my abilities and my mental toughness. I can't fully explain what exactly it was, but it was evident.

It was now 4th down and Coach Dennison called for the field goal team to go out and win the game.

Fank looked me in the eye and said, "You got this."

Nodding in acknowledgement, I jogged out, lined up my approach and signaled to Matt Shelton that I was ready.

"Easy chip shot. Go win the game brother," is what Matt said to me.

But making the kick and winning the game was the furthest thing from my mind.

The "what ifs" started coming out:

- What if I made the previous two kicks? We wouldn't even be in this situation.
- What if I miss this? Surely I'll lose my starting job.
- What if it's a bad snap?
- What if they block it?

The list goes on. Every negative thought you can think of in that situation, it was in my head. I was in my OWN head. Which is not the best place to be.

I wasn't poised. I wasn't focused. Quite the opposite.

And I missed. In fact, as soon as I hit the ball, I knew I missed and didn't bother to see where it went.

I let the pressure get to me. Heck, I let **my** own pressure get to me. After the game, a game in which we lost in overtime, I remember zoning out completely. I was ashamed, disappointed, and hurt. I knew I let everyone down and to be honest, it could've been a perfect time to throw in the towel and give up my football career. And it severely affected me mentally.

I carried that vision of that kick the entire season inside of my head and heart, and it absolutely tore me up.

In fact, it affected my personal life too, in ways that are difficult to understand. I felt so ashamed that I thought of quitting the team the following day and transferring schools, not knowing the amazing friendships, relationships and future accolades and experiences I would leave behind.

But I didn't.

I didn't quit.

I didn't spend the rest of my career moping around and feeling sorry for myself.

I kept working and kept going.

I kept my **poise**.

Poise under pressure doesn't mean you're always going to succeed in every given moment or situation. Poise under pressure isn't always measured by what you do in high pressure situations. It's measured by what you do **after** the fact, whether it's a positive or negative outcome.

Yes, I let the external pressure, and my own pressure get to me and had a suboptimal performance in this game and in previous games before that.

But it was the decision to keep my poise and keep going **after** that which set me up to be better in future games, seasons and finishing strong in my playing career.

I can tell you in confidence today that experiencing the failures and challenges of that season were some of the greatest things that could've happen to me. Those experiences are one of the reasons I can talk about the importance of poise under pressure and how vital that core value is.

We hear all the time in the sports world about the pressure to compete, to win championships, and to build a winning culture. But this profound pressure is everywhere, in everything we do, internally and externally:

- The pressure of being a great parent.
- The pressure to pay the bills and make ends meet.
- The pressure on the field, court or in any athletic venue.
- The pressure to get your lesson plans done for your students.
- The pressure to succeed in the operating room.

The list goes on.

Pressure can unlock the best version of you. Or it can burst the pipes.

As an athlete, whether it was college football or in the competitive Spartan or Ironman races I am in today, pressure situations are everywhere. I felt it all the time as a place kicker in high school and college, knowing the circumstance of each kick and punt. Today, I'm thankful for that pressure and the circumstances that came with it.

There were times I thrived off pressure and other times I let it get to me, not just within the game, but personally as well. I let it affect other areas of my life.

I'm thankful because I succeeded on the big stage, but also failed a lot. Most of those failures are the reason this book became possible.

Those failures allowed me to understand what poise under pressure means.

The failures helped me to work at and establish poise as a father, husband, son, coach, and teammate.

Keeping your poise when it doesn't go your way isn't just a fabricated statement.

It's a decision and commitment you have to make every day and in all areas of your life.

Keeping your poise means responding based on your core values and principles and not reacting based on triggered emotion.

- Adapting and overcoming the pressure versus losing your head.
- The "next play" mentality versus letting it sulk.
- Never too high or too low on emotion but staying even keel.

- Relying on your preparation for the moment you're in.

You owe it to yourself.

Pressure moments are all around. It's up to you on how you remained poised in those moments.

Stay alert. Be prepared.

Calm within the Chaos

It's 6:55 AM and a 90 degree morning in Delaware, Ohio on July 28, 2019.

2,600 people are at the start line getting ready to submerge in the open water of Delaware State Park, the first leg of Ironman70.3 Ohio.

Another two to three thousand people are standing by in anticipation of the chaos that's about to ensue.

There is a five second rolling start with five participants running into the water with little to no separation to the group that goes in after. Claustrophobia, personal space, and peace of mind all go to the wayside. Conversations among participants surround me. The crowd yells in sheer excitement. Music blares over the speakers. Anxious thoughts flood my brain, and I remind myself to stand confidently, even though I am less-than-confident on the inside.

You prepared for this moment months, sometimes years in advance. You've mastered the physical preparation, the nutrition and recovery routine and are ready to take on something you've never endured in your life.

Are you ready?

Among the chaos, subliminal conversation and loud music, there is a **focus.** It's a focus that stands so clear that no one, not even the devil himself, can steer me away from the level of commitment, standard of excellence and the persistent process that I am pursuing.

The focus I'm describing to you is my 27-year-old self getting ready to compete in my first Ironman70.3 race. At the time, I had no swim experience. I had only bought a road bike four months before, and my race experience was limited to just two half-marathons under my belt.

Everything about an Ironman70.3 race is hard. Every stroke, pedal and step you take can either make or break you. Such is life.

I completed the 1.2 mile swim, 56 mile bike, and 13.1 mile run with a euphoric final stretch of red carpet signifying that everything you want is on the other side of **hard.**

I paint this picture because there's a distinct level of focus that's required of you, on any given day and any given moment. There is a level of focus that requires you to dial into the process, adequately prepare for any and all things and let go of the things that take away your focus.

That was me on July 28th, 2019.

- I dialed into the 20 week training plan that was required of me, focusing on one training session, one moment at a time.
- I adequately prepared for all weather conditions, elements, and possible factors in the race—swimming in open water, biking steep and long hills, running in intense humidity, and mastering hydration to a T.
- And I let go of the negativity, criticism, fear, and distractions that would have taken away my focus.

Those three levels of focus created a euphoric feeling and atmosphere like I'd never experienced. Nothing else mattered on that day but what was right in front of me—one stroke, pedal and step at a time. I wasn't focused on how fast I finished, placing in my age group or simply beating the person next to me. I was intent on being all-in to the process that prepared me for the moment, the sacrifice it took to get me to this spot and the love and support that was there for me. I was relentless about operating at a high level, doing my best and finding ways to adapt to whatever was in front of me.

The process is never perfect, and rarely do you go through it unscathed, but that's how you become resilient, by overcoming the imperfect process, patching up the scratches and scars you endured and finding ways to get better. Missing kicks, enduring mental errors and having disappointing football seasons my sophomore and junior year of college didn't break me or tear me down. Those shortcomings and failures taught me how to respond the right way, adapt and overcome pressure and strive to be better. That Lake Erie game and the consequences that came from it didn't just happen *to* me, it happened *for* me. It was a difficult situation and time in my life that opened the door for me to get better.

Resiliency isn't a finish line. It's a never ending process of finding ways to get better, keeping your poise when things don't go your way and remaining diligent to your vision. It can no longer be just thoughts and words. It has to be defined focus and solitude which can take you to another level.

To establish next level focus and solitude, you need to work through the thoughts, actions and habits that drive your focus and affect your solitude. Repeat the good thoughts, actions, and habits. Remove the bad thoughts, actions, and habits. Or, maybe, forgive the people, places and things that take away your peace.

Staying calm within the chaos requires:

- Refusing to succumb to the negative chaos in the world.
- Staying prepared, relaxed, and well-versed in the classroom or on the field.
- Establishing solitude and responding the right way to situations in your business or at home.

- Keeping a level head and moving the needle in the operating room, construction site or office.
- Blocking out the noise, fear, and distractions in your mind.

Being calm before, during and after my first Ironman70.3 race didn't just happen. I prepared for it, harnessed my focus around it, maximized my time in training for it and utilized the right energy into it.

There's no material item, filter or attribute needed to create next level focus. You already have everything you need to focus, to remain calm in the chaos and to operate at a high level.

Now it's just a matter of doing it.

Get ready. Stay ready. Be ready.

Find a way!

Take Action:

In this chapter I talked briefly about repeating good habits, removing bad habits and the art of forgiveness for things that take away your peace. I want you to do ONE thing from each of those prompts. Then, I want you to repeat it continually, so that it becomes second nature to you and part of your routine.

1. Create a good habit that works for you and moves the needle. Repeat it.
2. Remove a bad habit that is tempting, but you know will be a positive change.
3. If you need to forgive someone or something in your life, knowing it's still on your mind, do it. Forgive the person or place. Or maybe, you need to forgive yourself?

Repeatable actions become habits. Consistent habits become your character. Character becomes your legacy.

Chapter 8

There's Always Another Level

Here we are. The final chapter in this book.

If you stayed with me throughout this book and picked up a few nuggets of wisdom, good habits or even thought-provoking quotes, I am happy about that.

"Your thoughts become your words.
    Your words become your flesh.

Your flesh become your actions.
    Your actions become your habits.

Your habits become your character.
    *Your character becomes your **legacy.**"*

I heard those exact words for the first time from Todd Durkin in 2017, but that mantra has become a staple in my life ever since. They've transformed who I am as a husband to Riley, father to Sloane, a son and brother to my parents and sister and ultimately, who I am as a coach, teammate, friend and man of God.

I say this because sometimes we have to redefine our legacy and what it looks like in order to get to the next level. Too often we let our job titles, credentials and educational degrees define who we are and the legacy we leave behind. Now, if that's the way you want to determine your legacy, that's great! But leaving your legacy doesn't have to be measured by the tangible accomplishments, material items and the amount of money you've made. Let it be about the fulfillment and joy you find in your life, the positive impact you have on others and the purpose you've been called to serve.

There's never a straight path to success or fulfillment and, more often than not, we're led in different directions. Sometimes we have a "fork in the road" moment of deciding which way to go. And sometimes, we are pulled away from the direction we're truly meant to go.

Redefining my legacy started with the foundation of going deeper and pulling out the best version of myself, like Todd demanded of me. That foundation of going deeper allowed me to discover my purpose, like Kelli Watson envisioned in me. And going deeper into my purpose challenged me to keep showing up, getting better and raising the energy of others around me. Doing the work consistently, like Frank Pucher ingrained in my mind.

Now, not all of us have those defining moments in our lives that create clarity in how we want to live, what we want to do and the environment we want to create.

So, allow me to provide a roadmap—something that has worked for me and hopefully helps you get moving in the right direction.

To make it as simple as possible, I boil it down to a 3-step process starting with the foundation and core of who you are, defining what you do and why you do it and then ultimately taking action on it.

3 Steps:

1. Create or Refine the Vision
2. Define the Mission
3. Take Action

Create the vision

Before we can create or live out our legacy, deep thought and visual imagery is required.

Plain and simple: What do you want out of your life and what does it look like?

If you're unsure how to start, use the "Core 4" exercise that you did at the end of the Chapter 3, provided by Frank Pucher:

A. What does your **health** look like now and in the next 5, 10, 20 years and beyond?
B. What do your **relationships** with your significant other, family, friends, and team look like?

C. How is **wealth** being defined for you, in this chapter and the next chapter of your life?

D. What do you want to **experience**? Where do you want to travel? What's next?

Your vision is your vision—no one else's.

If you have the vision to run the most successful business in your industry, create that vision and do the work.

If you have the vision to win the Golden Apple Award as a teacher in your school district, create that vision and go after it.

If you have the vision to be a collegiate or professional athlete, visualize and create that vision.

The list goes on. Legacy always starts with the deep thoughts you create and how you envision yourself carrying it on.

Define the mission

After deep thoughts and visual imagery, start speaking and writing it into existence. Put your thoughts to words and your pen to paper.

The mission is the cornerstone to every successful business and organization, defining the overall goal, the areas of impact and most importantly, the integrity.

We all know the mission statements of the school we attend, the company we work for or the non-profit organization we serve. But do you know your own personal mission statement? Do you have that?

My mission and purpose in life:

Find a way to utilize my ability to move someone's currently energy to a different level, powered by my investment of caring for others, seeing the good in people and showing compassion.

My energy, passion and ability to elevate is what I'm meant to do.

A shorter vision is, "Show up and make someone better."

That's who I am as a person, as a coach and as Tim Carter. That's my DNA and divine uniqueness.

So, who are you as a person, husband, wife, son, daughter, etc.? What core values define who you are and what you do?

Need help discovering your mission? Here's a good template for you:

- What do you find joy and fulfillment in doing?
- How can that serve other people? What problem are you solving?

Your mission and purpose statement doesn't have to be a long. It just has to make sense to you, define who you are and the impact you want to create.

Everyone has a mission. Everyone has a purpose. Your *thoughts become your words, your words become your flesh.*

Now, it's just doing the work to discover what that is.

Take Action:

The third step of defining your legacy needs no explanation—Get Moving!

You can read all the self-help books, listen to thought provoking content, acquire every certification and degree and know all the tricks of the trade, but, until you take action on any of those above things, those things are just thoughts, ideas, dreams and wishes. Let's call it immeasurable action.

In other words, you have to do something about it.

Creating your vision and defining your mission statement sound cool, but those steps mean nothing unless you act on it. And what better time to act than right now?

But why now?

Because there's always another level in everything we do.

Abraham Maslow's Hierarchy of Needs Pyramid gives us a blueprint on this idea of achieving self-actualization and different levels of needs, starting from the foundation and core of what we need and who we are and continuing to rise to the top level of the pyramid of our lives.

Self-actualization is just a fancy term for finding and creating the best version of you. To be the best version of you, it isn't enough to get to the top. You have to keep going and keep climbing higher because there's always more work to do and more to prove. There's always another level.

You need to **evolve**. I need to **evolve.**

Evolving requires change. It is not necessarily changing who you are, but rather, adjusting and adapting which requires focus and attention to detail, maximizing your time and utilizing your energy in the best way you can. Harnessing focus requires attention to detail on the things that challenge you to go deeper, not just with the easy stuff, but with the consistency of persistence (see Chapter 3).

Harnessing time requires you to maximize the time you have now and the opportunities to press on, and letting go of what no longer serves you.

Harnessing energy requires you to expend energy on the things, people or places that move you. And, to refute the opposite.

Before you can get to the next level, you have to do the hard things. And once you do the hard things, you have to keep doing them, consistently. Doing your best and elevating to the next level of your life requires choices—hard and uncomfortable choices. Most of those choices require a deeper and better version of you, challenging you to be at your best. And also, challenging you to refute the choices and habits that bring out the worst in you. You have a choice to tread into the unknown or retreat to the familiar. But only one of those choices allows you to get to another level.

In everything we do, there's always another level. Get up, get after it and stay after it. Stop waiting around for things to happen. Your best self is waiting for you to make a move.

Make the most of what you're doing and involved in right now. You don't get that time back.

Utilize your good energy in what makes the most sense to you. Don't waste it.

It can no longer be just thoughts and words. Those dissipate in the air, but actions are long-lasting.

Make the decisions you need to make.

Have the conversations you need to have.

Do the things you want and need to do.

Live the life you want to live.

Tell your story that needs told.

We don't get these moments back.

I'll leave you with this:

Time

Maximize it. Cherish it.

Utilize it to share the good. And share it with good people.

There's a time to step up and lead.

There's a time to step back and listen.

There's a time to step aside and let God do his work.

And then, among those three aspects, there's a time to step into something deeper.

Your Legacy.

How much are you allowing the possibility to happen?

Find A Way.

Quick Hitters

Below I've included some "quick hitters" from my social media page as some added motivation for whatever task you're undertaking, feelings or emotions you have, difficult conversations you're coming up on, or if you just need a psychological kick in the ass!

Iron Sharpens Iron

If you're in a position to make someone better, do it.

- Help the student understand the lesson plan
- Play outside with your kids
- Give your client/customer undivided attention
- Hold your significant other's hand
- Send the encouraging text
- Tell the people in your life you love them

List goes on.

We're all in a position to make people better. Don't wait. Do it now.

#IronSharpensIron

#GetAfterIt

Self-Awareness

Be aware and be prepared.

Asking for strength often comes with resistance. The resistance isn't against us, but rather, for us.

What we asked for is the opportunity and the challenge to be stronger.

#GetAfterIt

Peace

Before we establish peace, we need to work through the thoughts, actions and habits that take away our peace.

Repeat the good thoughts, actions and habits.

Remove the bad thoughts, actions and habits.

Or maybe…forgive the people, places and things that take away your peace.

Choice is yours.

#GetAfterIt

Best Self

Before we can be our best selves, we have to work through the things that challenge us to be at our best.

And, to refute the things that don't.

Choice is yours.

#GetAfterIt

Get After It!

Get up. Get after it. Stay after it.

Stop waiting around for things to happen. Time waits for no one, but your best self is waiting for you to make a move.

You already have what you need to move forward. Go get better.

Choice is yours…

#FindAWay #GetAfterIt

Iron Sharpens Iron

It's no secret that before we can be at our best, we need to be around the people that make us better.

The people that make us better are authentic and real, honest and forthcoming, purposeful and diligent.

They don't tell you what you want to hear, but what you need to hear.

No facade. Unfiltered. Divinely unique.

Go make someone better. You'll be better because of it.

#GetAfterIt

Courage

Before we can establish strength and courage, we need to work through our weaknesses and fears that precede being strong and courageous.

Be strong in your health.

Be courageous for yourself, family, inner circle, and team.

Be strong in doing the right thing.

Be courageous in knowing that the right thing isn't the easiest to do.

List goes on. Choice is yours…

Joshua 1:9

#GetAfterIt

Be Resilient

Before we can establish resilience, we need to work through the challenges, barriers and situations that create the breakthrough on the other side.

The physical, mental or emotional challenges you don't want to face…face them head on anyway.

The barrier that you think is blocking you…break it down anyway.

The uncomfortable situation you're in…get comfortable anyway.

You already know what you need to do. Get up, dust yourself off and go.

#FindAWay

#GetAfterIt

Unlocking the Next Level

Before we can unlock the next level, we need to harness our focus, time and energy.

Focus on the things that challenge us to go deeper. Not the easy stuff, but the consistency of persistence.

Maximizing the time we have now and the opportunities to press on. Letting go of what no longer serves us.

Giving energy to the things, people or places that move us. Refute the opposite.

You already know what to do.

There's always another level.

#GetAfterIt

Aligning Energy

Before we can establish next level focus, we need to align our energy to the right things.

Your morning routine that moves the needle.

The people you hang out with, work with and see often. Be self-aware and then, aware of the external.

Your stewardship and nourishment, of all things. What's your gut telling you?

List goes on…

The fourth quarter of the year and in life requires the next level of you.

Choice is yours.

#GetAfterIt

Focus

Before we can unlock the deepest version of ourselves, we need next level focus.

Zoning in on the task at hand. Commit to it.

Shutting out all the noise, negativity, fear, and distractions. Condition for it.

Doing the work that's required of you...and then some. 1 thing at a time.

Knowing you already have what you need.

Do what you need to do. And do it now.

#GetAfterIt

Establishing Solitude

Before we can establish the next level of patience and solitude, we need to work through the noise in our lives.

Poise under pressure.

Calm within the chaos.

Character outweighing criticism.

Will overcoming worry.

List goes on. Choice is yours.

#GetAfterIt

Find A Way Definition

Find a way means never being satisfied.

It's the understanding that there's always another level in whatever it is you do.

The constant battle of being at your best, knowing sometimes, you have to be better than your best. Even when you're at your worst.

Getting hit in the mouth and making the non-negotiable decision to get up, dust yourself off and go. Even when you'd rather lie down.

Reaching deeper into the well, even when it seems bare-bones dry.

Tap into the resilience on the other side…

Choice is yours.

#GetAfterIt

Do The Work

The standard is the standard. Show integrity.

The expectation is the expectation. Be diligent.

The work is the work. Do it anyway.

Hold yourself accountable. Raise your level of expectation. Be strong and do the work.

Thoughts and words are cool, but actions get it done. Every time.

The excuse used yesterday no longer works. Go get it done and then do it again. Over and over.

#GetAfterIt

Gratitude

It's no secret that gratitude can be one of the most fulfilling aspects of our lives.

But it's the moments after being grateful that move the needle.

Be grateful for family and friends by being a better family member or friend.

Be grateful for your health by improving your health. Physically, mentally, emotionally and spiritually.

Be grateful for the challenges and opportunities in your life by being great within those challenges and opportunities.

Gratitude isn't just thoughts and words…let's get better.

#GetAfterIt

"Anyway"

The best advice I've ever been given:

"Put your head down, shut up and work" - Falcon Hinkle

Things won't always go your way. Adapt anyway.

You won't always feel your best. Give your best effort anyway.

You're not always going to be motivated. Be disciplined and committed anyway.

Your message and good energy won't always reach people. Keep sharing, spreading good energy and being a good person anyway.

These prompts can no longer be just thoughts and words.

Don't wait until next week. Don't wait until January 1st.

Go do the work today. Do it again tomorrow. Do it every day.

#GetAfterIt

Solitude

Before we can unlock the solitude we seek in our lives, we need to hone in on our intangibles.

Awareness is key.

Poise under the pressure needed.

Repetitive action required.

Among all the noise and chaos there has to be a distinct focus.

A focus that stands so clear that no one, not even you, can take away your peace and solitude.

Lock in.

Be aware. Stay poised. Act on it.

#GetAfterIt

Iron Sharpens Iron

Iron sharpens iron isn't just a cool verse in the book of Proverbs and cliche term we use.

It's an embodiment of what we're called to do. Everyday.

The environment you choose to be in.

Who you hang out with, work with and train with…it matters. Everyday.

We get better by making other people better.

We get better when we're around people that make us better.

Check your attitude and energy…you'll know what's right.

You either add or subtract…

You want to get better? Go make someone better. That energy will always come back to you.

#GetAfterIt

"Feel Like"

Most of my best work has come on days I didn't feel like working.

My best coaching moments have come in moments I didn't feel like coaching.

My best training sessions and races have come on days I didn't feel like training or competing.

And the greatest joys and fulfillment in life came from moments I didn't feel like working through.

What comes easily, goes just as easily.

Don't rely on motivation and "feeling".

Be committed and consistent.

Do it anyway!

#GetAfterIt

Take Ownership

Before we can unlock the next level of our lives…take ownership.

Your health can be better.

You can develop great habits.

Your relationships can improve.

You can be a better student, athlete and competitor.

You can be a better parent, teacher, coach, medical professional, business owner, sales rep, etc.

The standard is the standard. It takes what it takes.

There's always another level.

#GetAfterIt

Acknowledgements

Todd Durkin

TD. The world is a better place because of your immeasurable level of impact and the unfathomable path God has placed you on in your life. From the first moment you coached me in August of 2017 and unlocked my best self, to the present day. I thank you.

To the best coach and mentor I've ever had, I thank you for your leadership, guidance, friendship, and the many "hand on the shoulder" moments you've provided in my life. #IMPACT

Kelli Watson

As I said in the book and to many of my peers—everyone needs a Kelli Watson in their lives. Thank you for your world-class coaching, unwavering leadership, love and support you've shown me in the time our paths have crossed. You have been a godsend in my life personally, professionally, and spiritually. Oh… and thanks for publishing this book.

Frank Pucher

Coach Frank, from the moment I met you at Rancho Bernardo Inn in February of 2018, you have told me what I NEEDED to hear and have coached me to continually show up, be consistent and get 1% better every day. You've inspired me to #DoBetter and to dial in on the little things that always add up. "More isn't better. Better is better" - #Frankism

Larry Indiviglia

Salute to you, Larry. For the many deep, personal and needle-moving conversations that you and I have shared over the last 6 years, I thank you. Whether the conversation was in Todd's living room in 2020 or the hotel lobby in Whitefish, Montana in 2023, it has been each of those conversations that presented lightbulb and pivotal moments which have led to impactful changes and transitions I have made over my career, personally and professionally. Health & Happiness to you, always.

Jill Rooks

My divine friend on the other side of the country, coach, and "foxhole" teammate. You continually inspire me to stand for something, to keep planting the seeds and laying the groundwork and are a constant reminder of the work God is doing in our lives. The example you lead by is remarkable, the change you've

Acknowledgements

created is admirable and the gratitude I have for you is formidable. #DoItAnyway

Julie Wilcox

Mama Jules, if they haven't yet, everyone needs to experience the energy and power of a Julie Wilcox hug. From the moment I walked into Fitness Quest 10 in February 2018, you've cared for me as your own and exemplified the literal meaning of being a leader in service to others. Thank you for your love, support, out of this world kindness and your smile.

Kim Wagler

Wags, for the opportunity to learn from you, coach with you and experience all of the many, memorable moments from that day walking into Impulse in 2016 as "crazy kid" to now, the impact of your guidance is unquantifiable. Thank you for continuing to elevate and challenge me as a trainer and coach, the mentorship you provided in many ways and for always welcoming Riley and I as family.

Brian Mong

Coach Mong, one of the turning points in my life, health and fitness was seeing how much you cared, perfected your role as a strength and conditioning coach and the diligent work you consistently put in to be the best in the industry. I knew then as a high school junior in

2009, and I know now and forever. You are the embodiment of resilience, true strength and building from the ground up. Thank you for leading my example and for trying to kill me on the freakin' Airdyne bike.

John Fankhauser

Coach Fank, from the day I met you at the Ohio State camp in 2010 until now, you have always demanded my best. The moment you recruited me to Walsh University, coached me every moment in my career, held me accountable as a colleague, whether on staff with you or in Admissions, and have continued to mentor me into who I am, I thank you.

Thank you for knocking me on my ass in March of 2012 and reminding me that there's always another level in who we are and what we do.

Mike Gallina

Mike, from Day 1 in the DeVille School of Business Mentoring program in 2012, to leading the blessing at our wedding and continuing our mentor/mentee relationship, your leadership and guidance has been second to none. I am grateful for your diligent work, the symbol you are to the entire Northeast, Ohio community and the consummate coaching you have provided me along the way. The big post it notes will always win out. *High Five*

Acknowledgements

Bonnie Miller

Bonnie, among all the great coaches and mentors I've had in my life, I consider you the first.

The first one to tell me what I didn't want to hear but needed to hear. The first one who made me cry (haha!) as a 7th grader who didn't want to re-do my English paper, but it was because you refused to let me succumb to mediocrity and average.

The first one who told me and showed me what "compartmentalizing" truly means and how to live it out accordingly, in all things. The first coach I trusted to make me a better student, athlete and human being.

The first one who taught me what the meaning of a mentor and friend truly means. I love you and thank you.

Anthony Schrock

My brother, the level that my physical and mental health is at currently and the new levels I'm always looking to unlock, I attribute to those legendary workouts we had at the OG Pack Performance Center behind the Circle K. You and Caleb pushed me to a level I never knew I needed. You helped unlock the grit, resilience and toughness I was in search of for so long. And all it took was "Iron Sharpening Iron", my hands bleeding for days climbing those ropes and the brotherhood stemming from our playing days at Walsh. Love always.

About the Author

Tim Carter currently serves as a Site Operations Specialist for the Ecommerce Department at Lane Bryant, a Coach and Trainer at Cleveland Clinic Akron General and is a board member for Compassion Delivered, which is a non-profit with a mission of providing high-quality meals at no cost to those dealing with life-threatening and terminal disease.

He is also a speaker, entrepreneur and now author.

He has been in the fitness industry for nearly 10 years as a strength and conditioning coach and trainer, served in higher education for undergraduate and graduate enrollment for 8 years and in retail for almost 2 years.

He is a 7x Ironman70.3 finisher, avid Spartan race competitor, former collegiate football player and coach at Walsh University, where he obtained his Marketing degree and Master of Business Administration.

His greatest ambitions in his life are his desires to help others and serve whole-heartedly in the fitness, health and wellness industry on all levels.

His greatest fulfillments in life are his wife Riley Carter, their beautiful little girl, Sloane and dog, Willie.

Connect with Tim

Social Media:

Facebook: https://www.facebook.com/tim.carter.357
Instagram: @tim_carter23
LinkedIn: www.linkedin.com/in/tim-carter-6380

Invite Tim Carter to Speak:

Tim Carter is a dynamic, high-energy coach and speaker who loves motivating people to get better. As one who dials in and lives life on all cylinders, Tim has a passion to help others unlock the next level of their lives through commitment, ability to connect and conditioning on all aspects.

If you, your business, organization or team are interested in having Tim speak on Next Level Mindset, Unlocking Your Best Self or Redefining Your Legacy, please contact him through email

Trcarter23@gmail.com

Donate to Compassion Delivered

Become a donor, sponsor or volunteer with Compassion Delivered 501c3.

Our mission is to provide high-quality meals at no cost to people suffering from life-threatening and terminal diseases in Stark County, Ohio.

compassiondelivered.org

From the Author

*Everything we do in life starts with a desire to help someone,
even if it's 1 person.*

That's how this book came into fruition:
The desire to help and make someone better.

*My parents raised me with a foundation to care for others,
show compassion and see the good in everything
no matter what.*

*The truest and most authentic desire and action
I have ever known.*

*We all have the foundation and core of who we are.
But the question remains:
How can I get better?*

*Find A Way: Unlocking Your Best Self is authentic and real.
Honest and forthcoming. Purposeful and diligent.
No façade, unfiltered and unique.*

Find A Way

*As much as this book is about me, my personal journeys and life lessons. It's all about **you.***

You have the power to be who you want to be and create the life you want to live.

Are you allowing the possibility to happen?

#FindAWay

Made in the USA
Middletown, DE
09 November 2024